Coffee Houses

of Europe

D1797281

Coffee Houses
of Europe

Introduction by
GEORGE MIKES

with 99 color plates

Photographs by
MANFRED HAMM

THAMES AND HUDSON

Any copy of this book issued by the publisher
as a paperback is sold subject to the condition
that it shall not, by way of trade or otherwise,
be lent, resold, hired out or otherwise circulated,
without the publisher's prior consent,
in any form of binding or cover other than that in
which it is published, and without a similar
condition including these words being imposed
on a subsequent purchaser.

© 1979 Nicolaische Verlagsbuchhandlung, Berlin
English translation © 1980 Thames and Hudson Ltd, London
Introduction © 1980 George Mikes

First published in the United States in 1983 by
THAMES AND HUDSON INC., NEW YORK
First paperback edition 1986

All rights reserved. No part of this publication
may be reproduced or transmitted in any form or
by any means, electronic or mechanical, including
photocopy, recording or any information storage and
retrieval system, without permission in writing
from the publisher.

Typeset in Great Britain by Tameside Filmsetting Limited
Printed in West Germany by Passavia, Passau

Contents

Introduction

Some years ago, during the coldest period of the Cold War, a Budapest newspaper attacked me for something I had written. It said that I should not be taken seriously because I reflected the spirit of the coffee house. This was meant as an insult; a contemptuous dismissal. I took it as a compliment and was proud of it. At last, I was recognized as a true son of the coffee house, a representative of its spirit. I never even hoped to achieve as much.

What is, then, this spirit? More precisely: what *was* that spirit?

*   *   *

There was a little-known Russian émigré, Trotsky by name, who during World War I was in the habit of playing chess in Vienna's Café Central every evening. A typical Russian refugee, who talked too much but seemed utterly harmless, indeed, a pathetic figure in the eyes of the Viennese. One day in 1917 an official of the Austrian Foreign Ministry rushed into the minister's room, panting and excited, and told his chief, 'Your Excellency . . . Your Excellency . . . Revolution has broken out in Russia!' The minister, less excitable and less credulous than his official, rejected such a wild claim and retorted calmly, 'Go away . . . Russia is not a land where revolutions break out. Besides, who on earth would make a revolution in Russia? Perhaps Herr Trotsky from the Café Central?'

It took some time – everything takes time in Austria – until the Foreign Minister learnt that there *had* been a revolution in Russia and it had, indeed, been made by Herr Trotsky from the Café Central.

Or take another example, much less dramatic but more recent.

Two popes – well, let's say two senior cardinals of Viennese coffee-house society and intellectual life (which come, more or less, to the same thing) – have recently celebrated their seventieth birthdays. First came Hans Weigel's anniversary. The whole of Vienna, the whole country and many people outside Austria celebrated this sweet and gentle man and charming writer, with the single exception of his bosom friend, Friedrich Torberg. The two had had some small quarrel and Torberg was annoyed. When asked by several newspapers to write a tribute to his friend he angrily declined. Soon Torberg's own seventieth birthday was reached. He opened *Die Presse* and there was a long, warm and generous article on him by Hans Weigel. Torberg read the piece, shook his head in disapproval and sent a telegram to Weigel:

WHY DO YOU MAKE IT SO DIFFICULT FOR ME TO BE YOUR ENEMY?

These two stories reflect the microcosm and spirit of Central European coffee houses. (I have taken them from Vienna, because it has long been the coffee-house capital of Europe.) There are the incestuous feuds; everybody is everybody's friend but everybody is also everybody's enemy. Everybody knows everybody else but assesses him about as accurately as the Foreign Minister assessed Herr Trotsky. Hostility, jealousy, hatred and intrigues are as close ties as love and friendship; indeed, they are interchangeable. The sharp wit of the Central European coffee house is also in Torberg's telegram: and so is its charming forgiveness and the obvious shrug of the shoulders, the wise – or superficial? – conviction that ultimately nothing is half as important as it seems.

I was born, bred, educated in coffee houses and lived most of my pre-British life in them. The coffee houses of Lisbon or Madrid, the cafés and bistros of Paris, the tavernas of Greece, the clubs and pubs of London have their own atmosphere and traditions. They are fascinating places but they are *places*. You go there with some purpose. The Central European coffee house is not merely a place; it is a way of life. As Alfred Polgar – a great pundit and wit of an earlier age – put it: it is a *Weltanschauung*, a way of looking at the world, by those who do not want to look at the world at all. Every profession used to have its own coffee house and its *Stammtisch*, the regular table of regular guests. Every shade, faction or sub-group of each profession had its own coffee house. There were coffee houses for writers, journalists and artists, and these were the most famous, because their members were, if not the most interesting, certainly the most articulate. In addition to the well-known tables of artists, there were coffee houses for textile merchants, dentists, horse-dealers, politicians and pickpockets, among many others. The world of criminals was as much subdivided as every other sphere. A mere pickpocket would not be accepted by the table of self-respecting safe-breakers any more than a small money-lender would be tolerated at the table of top bankers. Every budding journalist was called 'Mr Editor', every clerk or office-boy 'Herr Direktor' and every obscure individual with no background or status at all 'Herr Hofrat', Mr Court Counsellor. Once I heard a young man tell the headwaiter: 'You don't need to call me Herr Direktor any more. I've got a job now.' Not that the head-waiter did not know. He knew everything. You shared your secrets with him and even if you refused to share he knew them all the same. He lent you money when in need and lied for you when a persistent creditor pursued you. On the other hand, when a friend called he would not simply inform him that you were not there, he would tell him when you would return. He kept your letters for you: letters not meant for your wife's eyes were sent to your café as well as some totally innocent letters, because not everyone knew your private address but everyone knew which coffee house you frequented.

The coffee-house guest was no great lover of nature. 'Spring is here when the artificial trees are being put out on the terraces of the coffee house,' they said. They could not tell other signs of spring, nor were they interested. Hatred of fresh air, all sports and exercise was an almost universal trait in all true coffee-house-goers. They were no great lovers of home-life either. 'The coffee house has two great advantages,' said the sages of Central Europe, 'that you are not at home, yet you are not in the fresh air.'

'IT'S LIKE YOUR HOME', 'THIS IS YOUR SECOND HOME', and phrases like that were bandied about in coffee-house advertisements, but that was a misconception. People did not want their coffee houses to remind them of their homes; they wanted their homes to resemble coffee houses. Chancellor Raab – one of the post-war chancellors of Austria – had his office rearranged as if it were a coffee house, complete with marble tables. His newspapers had to be fixed on large wooden frames and he had two glasses of cold water put on a silver tray in front of him. He, as Chancellor of the land, could not very well go down to the café on the corner to do his work or receive foreign ambassadors there. But as a true son of Vienna he just could not work in any other surroundings. And this goes for all true sons of Central Europe. Bartók, Kodály, and Ferenc Molnár were regulars of Budapest cafés. No Viennese, be he Arthur Schnitzler, Sigmund Freud, Alfred Adler or Karl Kraus, could avoid the coffee house any more than a man living in Rio de Janeiro can avoid the sunshine.

*   *   *

It is surprising that the coffee house should have originated – at least as a European habit – from Vienna and not from Hungary. The coffee-drinking habit was brought to Europe by the Turks. Vienna was besieged by the Turks twice but never taken; Hungary was under Turkish occupation for a century and a half. Yet, the coffee-drinking habit did not take root in Hungary in those days. The Magyar peasants watched the Turks drink coffee at the end of each meal and were horrified. There is still a saying in the Hungarian language, 'The black soup is yet to come,' – a reference to the Turks' masochistic habit of inflicting the punishment of black coffee on themselves.

How coffee got to Vienna is quite a romantic story. In Vienna it is extremely difficult to find a true Viennese, or to put it differently – and more accurately – a true Viennese is a man of Czech, Magyar, Slovak, Ukrainian, Moravian or Macedonian origin, usually with an unpronounceable name. So it is most appropriate that the most Viennese of all Viennese institutions should have been founded by a true Viennese, who was – as he was almost bound to be – a Pole coming from Serbia, by the name of Koschitsky. During the second siege of Vienna, in 1683, he was moving around in the Turkish military camp, ostensibly selling coffee – an absolute necessity for the troops – but in fact spying for the Austrians. As a reward for his services (and to commemorate his method of collecting intelligence) he was given permission to open the first coffee house. The Café Koschitsky had six tables (marble tables, which have been obligatory ever since), four benches, six chairs, a big mirror and a portrait of the Emperor on the wall. There were newspapers on the table (people came in to read the *Wienerische Diarium*) and perpetual candlelight. Two cups of coffee, with sugar and whipped cream, cost 4 Kreuzer, with milk instead of cream 3 Kreuzer (less than a penny).

The Café Koschitsky was a great hit and other coffee houses were opened. In 1700 there were four coffee houses in Vienna; in 1747 there were eleven; in 1819 150, in 1873 200 but in 1910 there were more than 1200 of them. Their number declined during World War I because many of the guests were called away on other duties but by 1938 their number reached a record, 1283 altogether. After World War I banks were expanding; and as coffee houses, as a rule, occupied excellent venues, they were taken over by the banks. After the financial disasters of the Thirties, banks went broke and coffee houses reoccupied their former venues.

*   *   *

The coffee house flourished all over the territories of the Austrian Empire. Prague was as famous for its coffee houses as Cracow and the coffee houses of Trieste, Milan and Venice – once upon a time parts of Austria – were as different from the cafés of Sicily or Calabria as a Milanese banker differs from a *mafioso* (at least in outward appearance). Other Latin countries copied Central Italy, Spain and Portugal. The French cafés are different again, fulfilling an utterly different function. Amazingly, people go there to have a cup of coffee or a glass of beer; to have a short rest; to meet a friend. The French simply *use* the cafés; they don't *live* there. The cafés of the Champs-Elysées are different breeds once again. People sit down there to watch the passers-by and then, after a while, people change places: the strollers come in, the sitters go on parade. One group watched the other; now the other watches the first.

Talking of the coffee houses of the various nations, it should not be forgotten, of course, that the first coffee house city of Europe – preceding even Vienna – was London. The cafés were centres of political and literary influence, the meeting-place of the wits, philosophers and sages. Dr Johnson sipped there the cup that cheered (it was coffee in those days) and uttered his immortal *aperçus* at frequent intervals. Eventually the London coffee house declined: pubs and gentlemen's clubs took its place.

* * *

Why coffee house? Why not tea house? Or wine bar? How important is coffee in this context? Very important.

In a Viennese coffee house there are 28 varieties of coffee and all habitués, worthy of the name, let alone waiters, know them all. Indeed, more than all. I have checked once on these varieties with quite a few experts. The knowledge of some fell short; but the overwhelming majority could name more than 28, one went over 50. Yet, the sacred number is 28. Whether it is more or less, you must always speak of the 28 varieties of coffee just as you always speak of Ten Commandments and not nine or eleven (even if you remember the eleventh and most important: 'Thou shalt not be found out').

How on earth can they invent 28 varieties of coffee? a beer-, whisky- and tea-drinking Briton will ask in astonishment. First of all, you must decide on the amount of coffee you require: small, medium or large cup; some want it strong, others weak: short or long – that is, depending on the amount of water added; some want it in a glass, others order a little copper pot and pour out cup after cup for themselves; then you can have it light or in various shades of brownness; you may have it with milk or with whipped cream. (There is a story about the fussy guest who sent back the black coffee he had ordered because – he said – it was without milk, while he had ordered it without cream.) You may also describe the way you want your coffee prepared: you may insist on an espresso machine but many prefer more orthodox methods. You may order Turkish coffee. The vocabulary is rich: gold, nut-gold, nut-brown. Kapuziner (quite dark, a reference to the cassock of the Capuchin friars), or you may prefer the lighter brown of the Franciscans. You may want your coffee with rum, with whisky (Irish coffee) and even with an egg – served to the sick. (I thought you would serve coffee with an egg to someone you wanted to *make* sick.) You may order iced coffee or coffee with icecream in it, and so on and so on. There is only one order you cannot possibly give: 'A coffee, please.' That is utterly meaningless.

We have seen how coffee got to Austria from the Turks; but how did it get to the Turks? That is a bit of a mystery. We do know that coffee was familiar to the people of North Africa and Southern Arabia as early as the ninth century and started playing some part in their religious rituals, just as wine plays a part in Christian and Jewish services. A strictly orthodox section of Islamic priests decided that coffee-drinking was sinful because of its stimulating and intoxicating effect, so coffee became forbidden. The prohibition was not a success.

The name *coffee* is obscure. The Arabs called it *qahwah*, the Turks *kahveh* but some etymologists insist that the name comes from *Kaffa*, a town in south-west Ethiopia, which (according to some researchers, mostly Ethiopian researchers) is the birthplace of coffee.

Wherever it came from, it is here and it is warmly welcomed by many, myself among them. I have lived in England for more than four decades and I have got more anglicized than I care to admit. But I could not – and never will – come to terms with the English passion for the insipid, milky tea. I keep drinking coffee and miss the coffee house as much as Central Europe does because they are in decline; only a few survive as relics of the past.

The decline of the coffee house is caused mostly by lack of space. It has become economically impossible to let a person occupy a whole table by himself, stay there for hours at the price of a single black coffee (even with an egg in it), insist on getting two glasses of iced water every hour and to supply him with all the newspapers and magazines of Europe (and a few from the United States) into the bargain. Some survive because they are, in fact, restaurants disguised as coffee houses; others are subsidized by the city or by the tourist board for sentimental reasons or because they are tourist attractions; a few struggle on heroically and a very few even successfully. Well, time passes, institutions become outmoded and they die. But it is a great pity that the glorious, destructive yet civilizing spirit of the coffee houses is slowly dying with them.

Or perhaps it isn't. Perhaps Hans Weigel was right when he told me: 'The coffee houses were certainly decimated but not exterminated. The coffee-house industry is like the film industry. The film industry has certainly changed; there are fewer cinemas than there used to be but the film industry is still a powerful influence. So is the coffee house; it is immortal.'

*   *   *

Be that as it may, it *deserves* immortality.

Where are the places today where you can sharpen your wits in constant combat, be comfortably at home in the circle of your close and intimate enemies, hear all the gossip and be always on the alert lest your best friend stab you in the back with his tongue? No mercy was given or asked for; he who winced under attack only made himself more ridiculous and more vulnerable. If you could not attack anyone else, you made fun of yourself.

Ferenc Molnár, the brilliant playwright, a great success all over the world with the exception of Britain (although he is gaining some posthumous recognition even here), courted Sári F., the greatest and most dazzling star of the Hungarian operetta. The lady was an outstanding artist and had many virtues, but sexual abstinence, fidelity and discretion were not conspicuous among them. When Molnár returned to Budapest after a long absence, some of his coffee-house friends regaled him with stories about the lady's infidelity and told him that he ought to do something about it. She had gone to bed – his friends assured him – with every Tom, Dick and Harry.

Molnár shook his head and replied proudly,

'That's all right. She goes to bed with others because she loves them. But for money: only with me!'

This was the basic spirit – perhaps not altogether attractive but lively, warm, witty and just slightly murderous.

On a higher level, many great political and scientific ideas were born – or at least thrashed out – in cafés. Psychoanalysis, the great Compromise of 1867 between Austria and Hungary, as well as countless other famous schemes, were formulated and shaped in those smoke-filled rooms. The headquarters of the 1848 Revolution against Austria was the Café Pilvax in Budapest. Petöfi, perhaps the greatest among Hungary's many great poets, was a member of the *Stammtisch*. It was here that people formulated their revolutionary demands, the Twelve Points, and it was here that Petöfi first recited his incisive revolutionary poem, still learned by heart by every Hungarian schoolchild. That revolution in 1848 was inspired by poets and writers; so was the other in 1956, against the Russians. In those days Khrushchev remarked that if he had shot twenty Hungarian writers in good time, there would have been no Hungarian revolution. Probably true. But times had changed. That second revolt was not planned in coffee houses; tyranny and secret police-agents with long ears are as deadly enemies of the coffee house as changing economic laws.

Yet, the coffee house had its role and function on higher levels still. On one occasion a provincial priest was playing cards in the *Otthon* in Budapest – a journalists' club in name but essentially a coffee house – and was losing heavily. He was worried, he just could not afford it. Another blow seemed to fall: his opponent threw four kings on the table, a rare piece of luck which could only be defeated by four aces, an extremely unlikely combination. The priest kept his cards close to his chest, looked at them with agonizing slowness and in great trepidation. Noticing that he did have the four aces, he exclaimed,

'There *is* God in Heaven!'

The coffee house was the place for great and dramatic revelations; the place where four aces could resolve the tormenting doubts of provincial priests; the place where the ultimate truth would shine through. Alas, coffee houses are slowly becoming things of the past; so is the ultimate truth.

The Plates

ITALY

VENICE

Grand Café

Café Florian

23   Café Florian

Café Florian

Café Florian

Café Quadri

Café Tommaseo

Café Tommaseo

Café Tommaseo

Café Tommaseo

Café San Marco

Café San Marco

Café San Marco

Café San Marco

ROME

Café Greco

Café Greco

Café Greco

PORTUGAL

A Brasileira

A Brasileira

A Brasileira

Nicola

Nicola

SPAIN

MADRID

Café de Gijón

Café Comercial

Café Comercial

Café Comercial

BARCELONA

Café Zurich

Café Zurich

El Canaletas

El Canaletas

53   Café de la Opera

Café de la Opera

Café de la Opera

FRANCE

Café de Flore

Café de Flore

Café de la Paix

Café de la Paix

Café de la Paix

Le Carrefour

63   Le Carrefour

Pré Catalan

Grand Cascade

Le Dôme

La Palette

Aux Deux Magots

Aux Deux Magots

Aux Deux Magots

NANCY

Grand Café Excelsior

Grand Café Excelsior

Grand Café Excelsior

THE NETHERLANDS

Café Americain

Café Americain

Café Americain

GERMANY

Café Hennigsmeier

80   Café Hennigsmeier

MUNICH

81   Hofgarten-Café Annast

Café Venezia

Café Reitschule

84   Café HAG

Café Schapmann

Café Schapmann

Café Einstein

Café Einstein

Das Caféhaus (formerly Café Schilling)

Das Caféhaus (formerly Café Schilling)

BREMEN

Café Tölke

Café N.T.

Cron & Lanz

POLAND

CRACOW

Noworol

Noworol

Noworol

Jama Michalika

Jama Michalika

HUNGARY

Hungária

Hungária

103   Hungária

Hungária

Vörösmarty

Vörösmarty

Vörösmarty

CZECHOSLAVAKIA

Obecní dům

Obecní dům

Obecní dům

Slavia

Slavia

Slavia

KARLOVY VARY

Café Elefant

AUSTRIA

Café Sperl

Café Sperl

Café Sperl

Café Sperl

Café Sperl

Café Sperl

Café Hawelka

Café Hawelka

Café Hawelka

Café Museum

Café Museum

Tomaselli

Commentary on the Plates

The numbers relate to the pages on which the plates appear.

21 Grand Café, Venice, Piazetta. This café, occupying a part of the large San Marco 'café square', is situated in front of the Libreria Vecchia, a two-storeyed porticoed building with a statue-ornamented balustrade dating from 1536. It exemplifies the Mediterranean type of café open to the street and extending into the square itself.

22–5 Café Florian, Venice, Piazza San Marco. Founded 1720 and named after its first proprietor, this café is one of the most famous in Europe. Its present décor dates from the 19th century. In its heyday it was the venue of elegant Venetian and international society, and was patronized by famous artists and writers, such as Goldoni, Casanova, Rousseau, Byron, Goethe, Alfred de Musset, George Sand, and other celebrities of more recent times.

26 Café Quadri, Venice, Piazza San Marco. Founded 1725, it is, after the Florian, the most elegant café on the piazza.

27–30 Café Tommaseo, Trieste, Riva 8 Novembre 5. Founded about 1830 and called the Nuovo Tommaso after its first proprietor Tommaso Marcato of Padua. By slightly modifying the spelling, it became named after the Italian writer and revolutionary Niccolò Tommaseo in 1848. It was built in the style of coffee house common at the time of the Danubian monarchy, to which Trieste belonged until 1918.

31–4 Café San Marco, Trieste, Via Cesare Battisti 18. Founded 1914, it is one of the last remaining examples of coffee house characteristic of this era, with its marble-topped tables, bentwood chairs and billiard tables. At the beginning of World War I, it served as a meeting place for Italian nationalists agitating for an Italian Trieste. Because of this, it was shut down by the Austrian authorities, and not reopened until the war was over. Today the café is notable for its atmosphere redolent of the days of the Austro-Hungarian Empire.

35–7 Café Greco, Rome, Via Condotti 86. Founded prior to 1750, the earliest known documentary reference to it is one of 1760. It is named after its first proprietor Nicola della Maddelena, a Greek, and has numbered among its patrons Goethe, Schopenhauer, Mendelssohn, Liszt and Wagner, Stendhal, Thackeray, Gogol, Mark Twain, Bizet, d'Annunzio and Arturo Toscanini. The Greco acquired its present aspect around 1860, and since 1953 has been classified as a historic building.

39–41 A Braseleira, Lisbon, Rua Garrett 120/122. Founded 1904, this café stands today as a monument to the architecture of the turn of the century. Patronized by the poet Fernando Pessoa, among other literary figures, it remains a popular rendevous for Portuguese writers.

42–3 Nicola, Lisbon, Praca D. Pedro IV 24/25. Built in 1929 by the architect Norte Junior, the Nicola is a late example of Art Nouveau design.

45 Café de Gijón, Madrid, Passeo de Recoletos. Founded 1916, the Gijón is the best known of the Madrid cafés. In the 1930s, during the Civil War, when most other cafés had closed down, it became a meeting place for writers and artists,

initially from among supporters of Franco and then later those of the intellectual opposition.

46–8 Café Comercial, Madrid 10, Glorieta de Bilbao 7, was founded in 1911. One of its regular patrons was the poet Machado. The Comercial, a typical city café, has been owned by the same family ever since it opened.

49–50 Café Zurich, Barcelona, Plaza de Catalunya. Founded 1920, it is a popular daytime café patronized by young and old alike.

51–2 El Canaletas, Barcelona, the Ramblas. Founded in the 1920s, it is a combination of traditional café and modern-style café-bar.

53–5 Café de la Opera, Barcelona, the Ramblas. Founded at the turn of the century, it is built in Art Nouveau style. Situated close to the Teatro del Licco, it was once the venue of elegant opera-goers; today its clientele consists mainly of young Latin American émigrés and artists.

57–8 Café de Flore, Paris 6, 172 Boulevard St-Germain-des-Prés. Founded 1865, its style is Second Empire. Like the neighbouring café Aux Deux Magots, it was a favourite resort of artists and intellectuals such as Huysmans, Maurras and Barrès; more recently Sartre and Simone de Beauvoir frequented it.

59–61 Café de la Paix, Paris 9, 12

Boulevard des Capucines. Founded 1872, at the same time as the new Paris Opéra, and built in the same style, to designs by the architect Armand, it has now been added to France's list of historic buildings. With its marble pillars, contemporary wall and ceiling decoration, its ornate façade and antique furniture, it has come to be regarded since its renovation as a monument to the Second Empire's forte for ostentatious display. In its heyday it drew a wide clientele from kings and princes, poets and filmstars, to the demi-monde and the world in general.

62–3   Le Carrefour, Paris 11, 116 Avenue Ledru-Rollin. Founded 1902 and built by the architect Julien Galopin, Le Carrefour is a classic café-bar in the Art Nouveau style of the turn of the century.

64   Pré Catelan, Paris 16, Bois de Boulogne. Nestor Roqueplan's pavilion-like structure has undergone little change since it was built in 1905.

65   Grand Cascade, Paris 16, Bois de Boulogne. Napoleon III commissioned Baron Haussmann, Prefect of the Seine, who carried out a bold new plan for central Paris in the mid-19th century, to replace a 16th-century pavilion, and this elegant iron and glass erection was built on the original site. The Grand Cascade is a favoured venue of Parisian high society.

66   Le Dôme, Paris 14, 108 Boulevard du Montparnasse. Founded 1920, Le Dôme

soon made its name as an artists' mecca patronized by Picasso, Soutine, Dali and the like.

67   La Palette, Paris 6, 43 Rue de Seine. Opened in the 1920s, this café with its large-scale tiled murals depicting coffee-house scenes provides a documentary record of the ambience of those days.

68–70   Aux Deux Magots, Paris 6, 170 Boulevard St-Germain-des-Prés. Founded 1875, it is the most famous of Parisian 'literary' cafés. It derives its name from a business house which from 1812 on dealt in oriental merchandise and whose trade mark consisted of two grotesque Chinese porcelain figures (*magots*). Generations of the intelligentsia, artists and writers have forgathered here. Among the more famous with whom it has been associated are Verlaine, Rimbaud, Mallarmé, Breton, Artaud, Girardoux and Prévert. After World War II it became an existentialist centre with Sartre and Simone de Beauvoir in the forefront.

71–3   Grand Café Excelsior, Nancy, 50 Rue Henri-Poincaré. Founded 1904, this is a typical city café particularly favoured by Nancy's young intellectuals. In its décor it retains to this day the Art Nouveau flavour characteristic of the town at the turn of the century.

75–7   Café Americain, Amsterdam, Leidsekade 97. Like the Hotel American of which it forms a part, it was built at the turn of the century by the architect W.

Kromhout in Art Nouveau style. The leaded windows, sculptures and furnishings are the original ones, the lamps and murals dating from the 1920s. The building is on the list of Holland's historic monuments.

79–80 Café Hennigsmeier, Hamburg-Altona, Grosse Brunnenstrasse 60. Founded 1894, it is a classic *Café-Konditorei* situated in the autonomous urban district of Altona.

81 Hofgarten-Café Annast, Munich 22, Odeonsplatz 18. Founded 1810, it was incorporated sixteen years later into the newly erected bazaar building whose façade was designed by Leo von Klenze. It was named Hofgarten-Café Annast in 1920 after the proprietor Gustl Annast who took it over then. A few years ago the café was threatened with closure but strenuous protests by the citizens of Munich resulted in a reprieve.

82 Café Venezia (im Mövenpick), Munich, Lenbachplatz 8. The building of this former *Künstlerhaus* was conceived and financed by Franz von Lenbach, due to whose initiative it became a meeting place for artists. Some years ago it was turned into a restaurant. In a hall fitted out in the Italian style at the end of the 19th century to Lenbach's designs, the Café Venezia was incorporated into the Mövenpick. It is now listed as a historic building.

83 Café Reitschule, Munich 40, König-strasse 34. This café, founded 1928, was recently adapted in conformity with the Viennese coffee-house tradition, being equipped with bentwood chairs and marble-topped tables from the former Viennese Café Groppl. It forms part of the riding school premises.

84 Café HAG, Munich, Residenzstrasse 26. Founded 1825 as the royal *Hof-Konditorei* (Court Confectioner's), Rottenhöfen, it acquired its existing name when Peter Roselius took over the Palais.

85–6 Café Schapmann, Stuttgart, König-strasse 35. Founded 1925. Fitted out with period furniture and antiques, the Café Schapmann is a good old-fashioned *Café-Konditorei*, exemplifying the German café tradition.

87–8 Café Einstein, Berlin, Kurfürsten-strasse 58. Opened in 1978 and occupying an aristocratic town villa in Berlin's West End, the Café Einstein perpetuates the tradition of the Viennese 'literary' coffee houses. International concerts are given here from time to time.

89–90 Das Caféhaus (formerly Café Schilling), Berlin, Kurfürstendamm 234. Founded in 1902 and reopened after renovation in 1977, it is the oldest *Café-Konditorei* extant from the heyday of the famous Kurfürstendamm. At the time of its inauguration it was claimed that 'the wish to fit out the rooms in a style which should not pander to the mode of either the present or the future has led to a form that rests on the best classical foundation.'

91   Café Tölke, Bremen, Schnoor 23A, Am Landherrnamt 1. Opened in 1975 in a house dating from the turn of the century and fitted out in the Viennese style, the Café Tölke in the historic town centre is popular both with its youth and with the tradition-minded citizens of Bremen.

92   Café N.T., Düsseldorf, Königsallee 27. Opened in 1972, the N.T. was planned as a 'news café', with telex-secretary and other communication facilities, news-papers and magazines.

93   Cron & Lanz, Göttingen, Weender-strasse 25. Founded 1876, it is a good example of a traditional university town café.

95–7   Noworol, Cracow, Rynek Główny. Founded 1879 in the Cloth Halls of the main market, it was originally a confec-tioner's. This café, a meeting place for artists and writers, derives its present name from the second of its proprietors, Noworolski. The interior décor, dating from the time of 'Young Poland' around the turn of the century, is still partly preserved.

98–9   Jama Michalika, Cracow, ul. Flor-ianska 45. Of 19th-century origin, the café was refurbished in 1905 and enlarged by its then proprietor Jan Michalik in 1911. The entire interior décor of the newly appointed rooms, the paintings and furniture, were executed by Cracow artists in Art Nouveau style. The avant garde used to forgather in this café, and today it is still principally young people and artists who frequent it. Between 1905 and 1912 the politico-artistic cabaret 'The Green Balloon' was staged here; attempts have recently been made to revive this tradition.

101–4   Hungária, Budapest, Lenin krt 9–11. Inaugurated in 1894 as the 'New York' in a pretentious new building, it was renamed after World War II. The café, whose clientele included many Hungarian writers, among them Ferenc Molnár and Tiber Dery, as well as numerous inter-national celebrities, is still thought of as the 'New York' by the older habitués.

105–7   Vörösmarty, Budapest V, Vörösmarty tér 7. Founded 1858 by the master pastry-cook Henrik Kugler, it was taken over in 1884 by Emile Gerbeaud of Geneva, under whose name it became a famous confectioner's. It was renamed after World War II, but for the old people of Budapest the café with its 19th-century décor remains the 'Gerbeaud'.

109–11   Obecní dům, Prague 1, nám Republiky 1090. It was founded 1911, in the newly erected Prague House of Repre-sentatives and Concert Hall, the whole building with café and restaurant, in its architecture and interior décor, is pure Art Nouveau.

112–14   Slavia, Prague 1, Národní 1/1012. Founded after World War I, oppo-site the National Theatre on the bank of the River Moldava, the Slavia is a place where artists and writers, students and Prague high society all meet together.

115 Café Elefant, Karlovy Vary (Karlsbad), třida Dukelských hrdinů. It dates from the second half of the 19th century. The café, situated on Central Boulevard (former 'Alte Wiese') of the spa, maintains its traditional style. A guide book of 1888 says, 'Here feminine pulchritude and gracious charm combine with elegant taste to attract attention.'

117–22 Café Sperl, Vienna VI, Gumpendorferstrasse 11. Founded 1880, this café has faithfully preserved the aura of the Viennese coffee house of the 19th century, with billiard and gaming tables. Above all, it served as a venue for artists, who met one another here in the afternoons to play tarot, and were in the habit of scribbling caricatures on scraps of paper or even directly on to the marble table-tops.

123–5 Café Hawelka, Vienna 1, Dorotheergasse 6. It was opened in 1938 by Leopold Hawelka, who still owns it. After the end of World War II, it soon became a traditional coffee house, frequented by artists and literati, who moulded it into a successor of the legendary Viennese 'writers' café'.

126–7 Café Museum, Vienna 1, Friedrichstrasse 6. Founded 1899, the design and execution by Adolf Loos was in direct contrast to the ornate style of the period. Its original state has been only partly preserved. Before World War I the Café Museum was the meeting place of the Viennese avant garde, and it is still frequented by writers of all kinds.

128 Tomaselli (Kiosk), Salzburg, An der Residenz. Erected 1859/60 close to the Festspielhaus, the Kiosk belongs to the Tomaselli at Alte Markt 9, which dates back to 1764, and had already become a distinguished Salzburg café under its first proprietor Anton Staiger.

On the back of the jacket
Café de Chartres, now Restaurant Grand Véfour, Paris 1, 17 Rue de Beaujolais. Built in 1760 in the gardens of the Palais Royal, it was named after its owner, the Duke of Chartres. At the time of the Napoleonic Empire it was taken over by Jean Véfour and turned into a restaurant. The wall decorations of the inner rooms and the old name Café de Chartres on the façade were preserved.